I0002672

Copyright © 2015 by UI5CN

Rua Aquilino Ribeiro L280,

Pontinha, Lisbon

1675-292 PT

+351-968621883

www.UI5CN.com

1. The main category of the book — COMPUTERS > Enterprise Applications > General

TECHNOLOGY & ENGINEERING.

2. Another subject category — COMPUTERS > Web > Web Services & APIs

First Edition

Learn Simple

Free Gift Coupons

Or

Go here

You Might Be Also Interested In

Learn SAP® UI5: The new enterprise Javascript framework with examples

SAP® Netweaver Gateway: Learn how to use SAP® Netweaver Gateway for UI5 and ABAP projects

Data Visualization In 7 Simple Steps

Internet of Things with SAP HANA: Build Your IoT Use Case With Raspberry PI, Arduino Uno, HANA XSJS and SAPUI5

Table of Content

1. Introduction

What is D3?
D3 stands for Data Driven Documentation. It is a JavaScript library which allows developers to create amazing analytics and visualizations.

Why D3?
D3 should be preferred to any other JavaScript library, because there are a lot of options available for us. If we want to create some visualization projects like a simple project or a simple mathematical application then it is one of the best choices because of the following reasons.

Modern Browser Capability*:* We can use modern browser capability with D3. We have access to all the HTML5 and CSS properties. So, the created application is responsive and adaptable to user devices.

Endless Variations*:* Variations and options provided by D3 are endless. We will see in d3js.org website for possibilities of D3.

BSD Open Source License: D3 comes with a BSD open source license. So we don't need to pay anyone to use D3.

Large Community Support*:* D3 has large community support. There are lot of people in **StackOverflow** and **GitHub**. Support is essential if we are learning a new technology. This community will guide us to resolve any queries and issues that we face in projects.

Let's explore d3js.org website

If you go to the examples tab you can see popular examples in the gallery. Here we can see a lot of examples created using D3. There are many common graphs like Box plot, Bubble chart, Heat maps and more innovative charts like graph with force layout and motion charts are available in the examples tab. We will find several variations and innovative approach to solve any visualization problem using D3. In the right hand side, they have provided the API reference. It is very useful if you are new to D3. It contains the documentations and features of all elements used in D3.

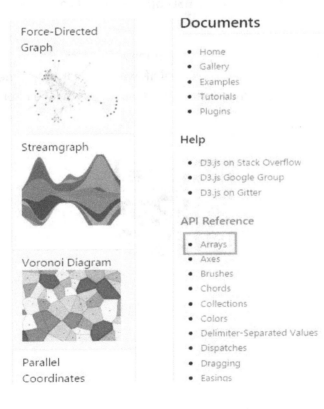

Arrays (d3-array)

Array manipulation, ordering, searching, summarizing, etc.

↻ Statistics

Methods for computing basic summary statistics.

- d3.min - compute the minimum value in an array.
- d3.max - compute the maximum value in an array.
- d3.extent - compute the minimum and maximum value in an array.
- d3.sum - compute the sum of an array of numbers.
- d3.mean - compute the arithmetic mean of an array of numbers.
- d3.median - compute the median of an array of numbers (the 0.5-quantile).
- d3.quantile - compute a quantile for a sorted array of numbers.
- d3.variance - compute the variance of an array of numbers.
- d3.deviation - compute the standard deviation of an array of numbers.

API Reference

Let's go back to the example and select one example to explore. Here we select the Box plot example to explore.

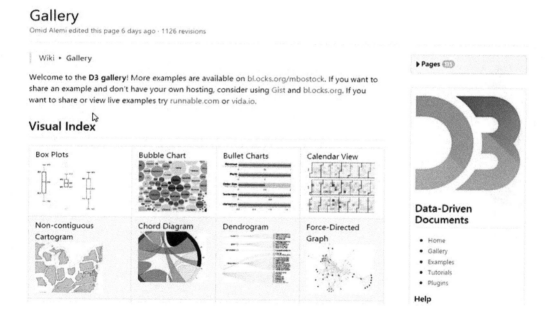

After selecting the Box plot, it opens the D3 example and the coding that created to the graph. Mike Bostock is the developer who created this graph. He also posted lot of examples. You can click his name to see the graphs posted by him.

Box Plots

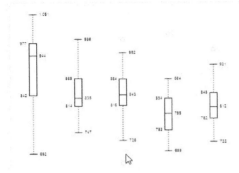

A box-and-whisker plot uses simple glyphs that summarize a quantitative distribution with five standard statistics: the smallest value, lower quartile, median, upper quartile, and largest value. This summary approach allows the viewer to easily recognize differences between distributions. Data from the Michelson–Morley experiment. Implementation contributed by Jason Davies. This example periodically randomizes the values to demonstrate transitions.

Open

index.html

```
<!DOCTYPE html>
<meta charset="utf-8">
<style>

body {
  font-family: "Helvetica Neue", Helvetica, Arial, sans-serif;
```

You can also check our **Learn D3.JS Hands-on And The Simple Way** video course for accelerated learning: here or use the below QR code for 50-90% off.

Learn D3.JS Hands-on And The Simple Way
UI5 Community Network • SAP Experts · SAP Services, SAP Consulting, SAP Education

Learn how to work with D3 Javascript libraries in step-by-step and most simple manner with lots of hands-on examples

● 35 lectures ⏱ 7 hours ||| All Levels

★ ★ ★ ★ ★ 4.4
(10 ratings)

2. LEARNING PATH OF THIS BOOK

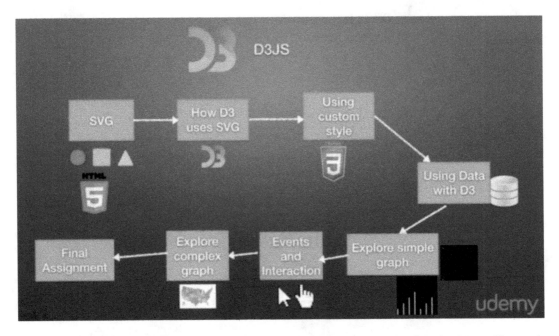

- Initially we will start with SVG (Scalable Vector Graphics). We will see how to create simple graphic objects like circles, rectangles and triangles.

- Also, we learn how these SVG elements can be drawn from HTML5. Next, we will use D3 to create these SVG elements.

- Once we get basic understanding the basic SVG elements works then we move on to work with custom style sheets (CSS).

- Working with CSS, we see how to use Data with D3.

- Following that we shall see how to use simple graph like bubble chart and bar chart.

- Then, we will see the Events in our graph while the end user moves mouse over the graph.

- Our learning curve would also proceed to some advanced graphs like map or heat map project.

- Finally, we will create an assignment project. This assignment will be a use case of a visualization project that we will solve using D3. We are going to learn the process step wise and by hands-on basis.

3. SVG Elements

SVG is a short form for Scalable Vector Graphics. Similar to PNG or JPEG files, SVG is used to store XML based vector image formats. A normal bitmap image is composed of a fixed set of pixels. A vector image, on the other hand, is composed of fixed set of shapes like circles, line or text. We can see that the image represented in .jpeg, .png or .gif files are pixilated or distorted. However, in vector images they are set of shapes and we would not see any quality compromise while zooming on the image.

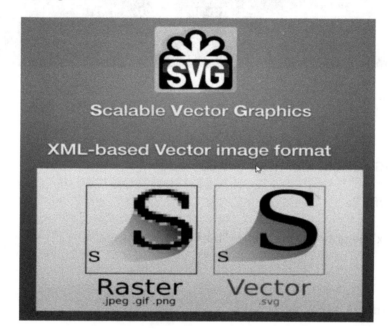

Examples

Let us see some simple examples of using SVG elements in our HTML5 page. We are going to use the Cloud9 IDE. We do majority of our developments in Cloud9 IDE. The files are accessible for our users 24x7.

Link for the repositories: https://ide.c9.io/ajaytech/dataviz

People who are not familiar with this IDE can read the document on getting started in the given link.

Getting Started: https://docs.c9.io/docs/getting-started

Let us **START CODING!**

3.1. Simple Example for SVG

In this example we are going to create a bar using SVG elements. To create a SVG, we need a <svg> tag. In this tag, we added the width, height and the background colours of the rectangle bar. If we add the below code before the body tag and run the code we will get an orange colored rectangle with width of 300px and height of 100px.

Code for SVG.html

```
<!DOCTYPE html>

<title>Create a SVG element with HTML and D3</title>

<meta charset="utf-8 ">

<svg width="300px" height="100px" style="background:orange">

</svg>

<script src="../D3/d3.v3.min.js"></script>

<script>

    var svg = d3.select("body").append("svg").style("background","green");

</script>

<body>

</body>

</html>
```

Result:

This is our **SVG** element. In future sections we are going to use it with D3.

body 607.3611450195312px x 173.333343505859938px

In this example we are going to use SVG element with D3. To do that, we need to use d3.select("body").append("svg"). The final hierarchy of our webpage will have a HTML element and inside that we will have a body and this body will contain the SVG element.

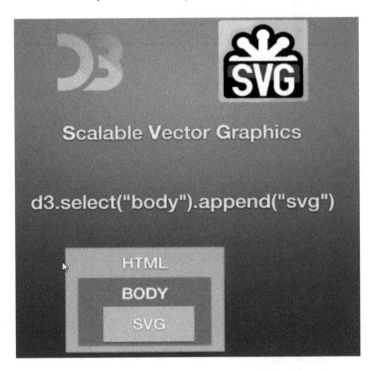

Let's try this out in our Cloud9 IDE. We already created a simple SVG element inside our HTML page. Now we are going to use D3 to perform the same activity. To use D3 we need to add D3 libraries before the body tag. To do that we need to add the link to that library inside the script tag.

<script src="../D3/d3.v3.min.js"></script>

<script>

The "../D3/d3.v3.min.js" is the relative path for D3 library files.

To verify this, run the file and go to console by right click on the page and select inspect element. Then, enter D3 and hit enter. If everything is perfect, then it does not show any errors and our path is correct.

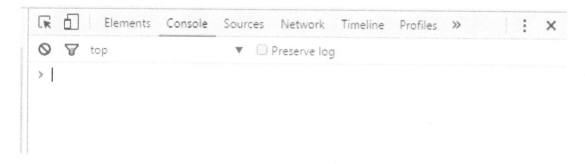

If there is some error in defining the path, then it shows like this in the console.

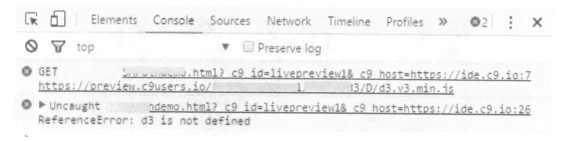

When we are working in a project we will always use the relative path or a path from a content delivery network CD. If we open the D3 library file then we will see a very big file inside it. This is the library file that we are going to use in our application. D3 is JavaScript based so we have a script tag and we write the JavaScript code inside the Script tag. The first example we are going to create is an SVG using D3.

Code for SVG with D3:

```
<!DOCTYPE html>
<title>Create a SVG element with HTML and D3</title>
<meta charset="utf-8 ">
<svg width="300px" height="100px" style="background:orange">
</svg>


<script src="../D3/d3.v3.min.js"></script>
<script>
   /*Creating a SVG inside the body and added style as green to make the SVG visible*/


   var svg = d3.select("body").append("svg").style("background","green");
```

```
</script>
<body>
</body>
</html>
```

Output:

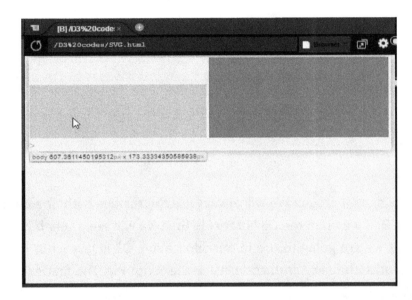

The first orange colored rectangle is without D3 and the second rectangle box is rendered by D3 syntax.   This is a simple example using SVG. We shall see a few more examples of graphic elements and its variations in coming sections.

You can also check our **Learn D3.JS Hands-on And The Simple Way** video course for accelerated learning: <u>here</u> or use the below QR code for 50-90% off.

Learn D3.JS Hands-on And The Simple Way

UI5 Community Network • SAP Experts · SAP Services, SAP Consulting, SAP Education

Learn how to work with D3 Javascript libraries in step-by-step and most simple manner with lots of hands-on examples

⭐ ⭐ ⭐ ⭐ ⭐ 4.4
(10 ratings)

⊙ 35 lectures   ⏱ 7 hours ||| All Levels

4. Selecting elements and operating

Similar to JQuery, if we like to hold on an object to make some changes or read some values we need to use select statement. D3 provides two top level elements for selecting elements **'select'** and **'selectAll'**. Let's start with select. In this example, we are going to have a simple HTML page that contains a body and this body will have a SVG element inside it. This SVG element will be containing some attribute values like width or height. These properties are actually called SVG properties.

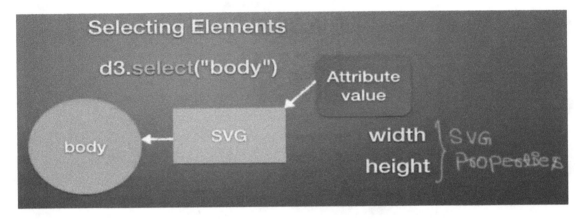

4.1 Coding

You have access to the repositories of these examples. To access it go to the link **https://ide.c9.io/ajaytech/dataviz**

We see the select and selectAll properties in this example. If we use the select property, it selects the specific elements that are mentioned. The first orange colour rectangle is the example for select property. The Dinosaurs, Elephant and Cat are used with selectAll. Here you can see that Dinosaur and Elephant are of green colour because in the div tag with id and class attributes we defined the background colour as green.

```
<script>
    var svg = d3.select("body").append("svg").attr("width","300px")
              .attr("height","100px").style("background","orange");


</script>
<div id="demo">Dinosaurs</div>
<div class="demoClass">Elephant</div>
<div>Cat</div>

<script>
    d3.selectAll("div").style("background","orange");

    d3.select("#demo").style("background","green");
      d3.select(".demoClass").style("background","green");
```

1. d3.select("body") is a jQuery selector statement that selects the contents inside body. The attributes are also defined here with style as orange background.

2. Div element with id demo and another div element with class as 'demoClass' are used to group the specified class or id.

3. The 'SelectAll' will select the entire SVG inside div and the 'Select' selects only the particular class or id that is specified inside the function.

Code for D3SVG.html

<!DOCTYPE html>

<meta charset="utf-8">

<title>Adding attributes and selection to SVG element</title>

<body>

<script src="../D3/d3.v3.min.js"></script>

<script>

   var svg = d3.select("body").append("svg").attr("width","300px")

       .attr("height","100px").style("background","orange");

```
</script>

<div id="demo">Dinosaurs</div>

<div class="demoClass">Elephant</div>

<div>Cat</div>

<script>

 d3.selectAll("div").style("background","orange");

d3.select("#demo").style("background","green");

d3.select(".demoClass").style("background","green");

</script>

</body>

</html>
```

Output

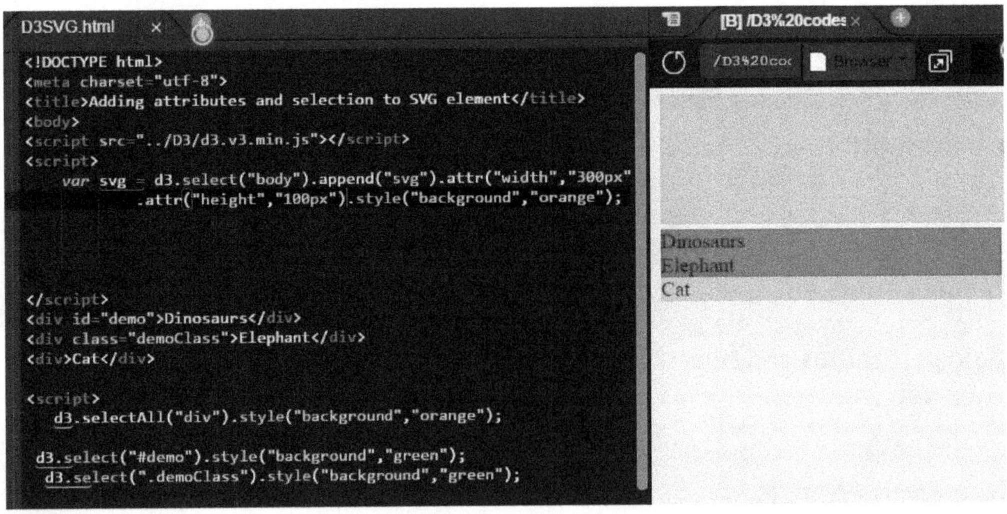

If we remove the id and class for the Dinosaur and Elephant and the actual result will appear as shown below.

```
<title>Adding attributes and selection to SVG
<body>
<script src="../D3/d3.v3.min.js"></script>
<script>
    var svg = d3.select("body").append("svg"
            .attr("height","100px").style("ba


</script>
<div>Dinosaurs</div>
<div>Elephant</div>
<div>Cat</div>

<script>
    d3.selectAll("div").style("background","or

 d3.select("#demo").style("background","green
  d3.select(".demoClass").style("background",
```

Dinosaurs
Elephant
Cat

You can also check our **Learn D3.JS Hands-on And The Simple Way** video course for accelerated learning: <u>here</u> or use the below QR code for 50-90% off.

Learn D3.JS Hands-on And The Simple Way

UIS Community Network • SAP Experts · SAP Services, SAP Consulting, SAP Education

Learn how to work with D3 Javascript libraries in step-by-step and most simple manner with lots of hands-on examples

○ 35 lectures   ⏱ 7 hours   ┊┊┊ All Levels

★ ★ ★ ★ ★ 4.4
(10 ratings)

5. Styling

Styling mostly refers to the CSS part of our D3 Application. The CSS part will make our application look nice. In addition, while we are drawing the graphical elements like bubble chart and bar chart, styling also becomes very essential when we differentiate the data points. Styling to our D3 can be achieved in three different ways.

- **Inline**

- **External**

- **Internal**

Inline

The rule of styling is to be within the quote ("").

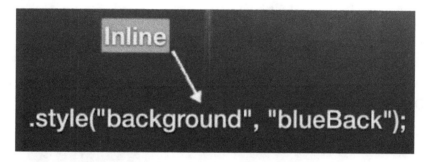

This is the Inline style rule that we saw in the previous example.

```
var svg = d3.select("body").append("svg").attr("width","300px")
            .attr("height","100px").style("background","orange");
```

External or Internal Style Sheet

In this scenario, the style is directly added to our element. However, the better approach is to go with the external or internal style class. Here we shall be defining a class and we will add this class to the element. Later on, if we want to change the properties then we don't have to access all individual elements to perform those changes. We simply do the changes in the class and it can be picked up by the elements of the assigned class. We will see this in our coding.

Internal Style Rule

The internal style rule can be defined inside the main coding without any external style sheets. The following code is an example for internal style sheet.

Code for Internal Style Rule:

```
<!DOCTYPE html>

<meta charset="utf-8">

<title>Adding attributes and selection to SVG element</title>

<style>

    .blueBack{          /* Class name blueBack containing the CSS property of blue colour. This is
                                                                     internal style rule

    background : blue;

}

</style >


<body>

<script src="../D3/d3.v3.min.js"></script>

<script>


var svg =
d3.select("body").append("svg").attr("width","300px").attr("height","100px").attr("class","blue
Back");

/* we are appending the class property 'blueBack' with body elements*/

</script>

</body>

</html>
```

Output

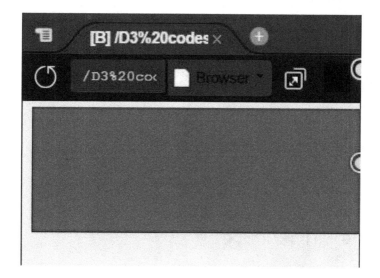

External Style Rule

External style rules can be added to the program by creating a <filename>.css file and link the CSS file inside the program. For instance, we create a style sheet as style.css then we link it in the program using the filename style. This can be linked at the start of the coding part shown in the following screenshot.

```html
<!DOCTYPE html>
<meta charset="utf-8">
<title>Adding attributes and selection to SVG element</title>
<link rel="stylesheet" type="text/css" href="style.css"></link>

<body>
<script src="../D3/d3.v3.min.js"></script>
<script>
    var svg = d3.select("body").append("svg").attr("width","300px")
        .attr("height","100px").attr("class","blueBack");



</script>
</body>
</html>
```

D3.Styling.html

```html
<!DOCTYPE html>
<meta charset="utf-8">
<title>Adding attributes and selection to SVG element</title>
<link rel="stylesheet" type="text/css" href="style.css"></link>

<body>
<script src="../D3/d3.v3.min.js"></script>
<script>
    var svg = d3.select("body").append("svg").attr("width","300px")
        .attr("height","100px").attr("class","blueBack");
</script>
</body>
</html>
```

style.css

```css
.blueBack{

    background : blue;

}
```

You can also check our **Learn D3.JS Hands-on And The Simple Way** video course for accelerated learning: <u>here</u> or use the below QR code for 50-90% off.

Learn D3.JS Hands-on And The Simple Way

UI5 Community Network • SAP Experts - SAP Services, SAP Consulting, SAP Education

Learn how to work with D3 Javascript libraries in step-by-step and most simple manner with lots of hands-on examples

⊙ 35 lectures   ⊙ 7 hours   �Ⅲ All Levels

★★★★★ 4.4
(10 ratings)

6. Geometrical objects

While we are creating a graph or chart, the individual elements of these graphs or charts are our geometrical objects. It can be a rectangle or circle and it can be a line or an arc. Let's see the example to make these geometrical objects using D3. In the previous section we saw how to add style sheets to our D3. In the same example, we will add our geometrical objects to it. In this example we are going to use the same SVG and append the rectangle inside it.

```html
<!DOCTYPE html>
<meta charset="utf-8">
<title>Adding attributes and selection to SVG element</title>
<link rel="stylesheet" type="text/css" href="style.css"></link>

<body>
<script src="../D3/d3.v3.min.js"></script>
<script>
    var svg = d3.select("body").append("svg").attr("width","300px")
            .attr("height","100px").attr("class","blueBack");

    svg.append("rect")
    .attr("width","100px")
    .attr("height","50px")
    .attr("x","100px")
    .attr("y","20px")
    .style("fill","orange");

    svg.append("circle")
    .attr("r","20px")
    .attr("cx","100px")
    .attr("cy","20px")
    .style("fill","green");
```

The code given below is to draw rectangle of size 100X50 pixels with padding x and y as 100 and 20 respectively. The **padding** is used to denote the D3 to start drawing the object in x and y axis. We also filled the rectangle with orange colour.

```
svg.append("rect")

.attr("width","100px")

.attr("height","50px")

.attr("x","100px")

.attr("y","20px")

.style("fill","orange");
```

The code to draw circle is given below. To draw a circle we need radius so we defined radius of 100px. The x and y is for the same purpose of padding in the rectangle. The colour inside the circle is given green to differentiate it from rectangle.

```
svg.append("circle")
        .attr("r","20px")
        .attr("cx","100px")
        .attr("cy","20px")
        .style("fill","green");
```

Code for D3GeometricalShape.html

```
<!DOCTYPE html>
<meta charset="utf-8">
<title>Adding attributes and selection to SVG element</title>
<link rel="stylesheet" type="text/css" href="style.css"></link>

<body>
<script src="../D3/d3.v3.min.js"></script>
<script>
   var svg = d3.select("body").append("svg").attr("width","300px")
        .attr("height","100px").attr("class","blueBack");



        svg.append("rect")
        .attr("width","100px")
        .attr("height","50px")
        .attr("x","100px")
        .attr("y","20px")
```

```
.style("fill","orange");

svg.append("circle")
.attr("r","20px")
.attr("cx","100px")
.attr("cy","20px")
.style("fill","green");
```

```
</script>
</body>
</html>
```

Output

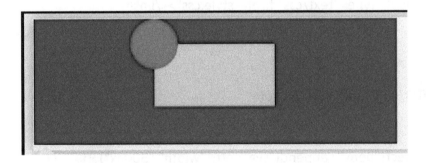

In real projects we use variables instead of hard coding the attribute values width, height. In the next section we will see bar chart using rectangles.

You can also check our **Learn D3.JS Hands-on And The Simple Way** video course for accelerated learning: <u>here</u> or use the below QR code for 50-90% off.

Learn D3.JS Hands-on And The Simple Way

UIS Community Network • SAP Experts - SAP Services, SAP Consulting, SAP Education

Learn how to work with D3 Javascript libraries in step-by-step and most simple manner with lots of hands-on examples

★★★★★ 4.4
(10 ratings)

● 35 lectures   ⊙ 7 hours   �ⅠⅠⅠ All Levels

7. Bringing Data into the Picture

We are going to use data into our project. The data can be JavaScript Array, JSON, XML or CSV Data. We can load the data to our D3 application externally. In real projects data will be passed to the application using Asynchronous request. We will be using some asynchronous services and via AJAX calls we will be getting the data to our application. In the previous section we saw geometrical objects. Using that we will create bar charts with some data to visualize in D3. There will be some new functions that we will see in our application called:

1. data()

2. enter()

We will discuss it in our examples.

Coding

We will create a new file named as **D3DataHand.html** and copy the structure from the previous examples and remove the other unwanted coding. Now, we are going to add some data using a variable called data. After adding data we will set the height and width of the total SVG. Also we are appending the SVG inside the body. Here you can see as we told in the previous section, instead of hard coded value we assigned the variables widthSVG and heightSVG. Also, we gave the background style as black colour.

```
var data=[10,20,30,40,100];
var heightSVG = 700;
var widthSVG = 700;
var svg = d3.select("body")
            .append("svg")
            .attr("width",widthSVG)
            .attr("height",heightSVG)
            .style("background","black");
```

After initializing the data we start adding data and draw our bar chart.

```
svg.selectAll()
.data(data)
.enter()
.append("rect")
.attr("height",function(d,i){
    return d*100;
})
.attr("width","20px")
.style("fill","orange")
.attr("y",function(d,i){
    return heightSVG -(d)*10 ;
})
.attr("x",function(d,i){
    return i*40;
});
```

- We are adding the data to the program using .data(data).

- After that, we use .enter() function. It is used to perform same actions to all data after enter(). It is similar to loop.

Then we will add rectangle. This rectangle width is constant but the height is dependent upon the data input. To make the height depend upon the data we add the function (d,i) where 'd' is the data and 'i' is the index. The width of the bar is constant because we are using bar chart here. So we gave the constant 20px. For the y value the function d and i are used to draw the rectangle according to the data. The returnheightSVG – (d)*10; is used to return the height of SVG according to the data. The value 10 is used for scaling purpose to enlarge or decrease the size of the rectangle.

Code for D3DataHand.html

```
<!DOCTYPE html>
<meta charset="utf-8">
<title>Adding attributes and selection to SVG element</title>
<link rel="stylesheet" type="text/css" href="style.css"></link>


<body>
<script src="../D3/d3.v3.min.js"></script>
<script>
```

```javascript
var data=[10,20,30,40,100];   //Data variable Array
var heightSVG = 700;          //Maximum height of SVG
var widthSVG = 700;           //Maximum width of SVG
var svg = d3.select("body")
      .append("svg")
      //As we told in previous example we removed the hard coded value and given variables
                                                           widthSVG and heightSVG


      .attr("width",widthSVG)
      .attr("height",heightSVG)
      .style("background","black");  //Black background

      svg.selectAll()
      .data(data)      //Passing the data here
       .enter()        //This will do all the things after this code for all the data points
      .append("rect")    //Append rectangle
       .attr("height",function(d,i){  //Adding height using function depending upon the data.
        return d*100;
      })
                                    .attr("width","20px")//Fixed width because of bar chart
      .style("fill","orange")
      .attr("y",function(d,i){
           return heightSVG -(d)*10 ; //Subtracting the data from total heightSVG. 10 will
                                                           increase the scale of the bar


      })
      .attr("x",function(d,i){
        return i*40;
      });
</script>
</body>
</html>
```

Output:

You can also check our **Learn D3.JS Hands-on And The Simple Way** video course for accelerated learning: here or use the below QR code for 50-90% off.

Learn D3.JS Hands-on And The Simple Way

UIS Community Network • SAP Experts - SAP Services, SAP Consulting, SAP Education

Learn how to work with D3 Javascript libraries in step-by-step and most simple manner with lots of hands-on examples

⚫ 35 lectures   🕒 7 hours   ┊┊┊ All Levels

★ ★ ★ ★ ★ 4.4
(10 ratings)

8. Loading Data from external file

Loading data from external file may be in CSV, JSON or TSV formats. We are having a simple D3 function that will load data from these external files. The function is:

```
d3.csv("filePath",function(data){

    })
```

The first parameter is path of the filename and second parameter is the function that will be executed once the data is loaded from the file. Let's start coding for a better understanding this example. In previous example we use data internally. We can use data externally by doing some simple changes in the code.

Create a new file **D3DataLoad.html** and copy the code from previous example. Remove the values we defined previously. In addition, we need to create one more file called **data.csv** . It is used to store our external data. We add some data into that as 10, 20, 30, 40, 20, 10, 100.

Let's create some bar chart using these values. Now we are going to use the d3.csv("data.csv",function(d){} function to add the csv file. We also add a function for error in case of any issue in or file then it will clarify it in the browser console. These are changes we did from previous example.

```
<!DOCTYPE html>
<meta charset="utf-8">
<title>Adding attributes and selection to SVG element</title>
<link rel="stylesheet" type="text/css" href="style.css"></link>

<body>
<script src="../D3/d3.v3.min.js"></script>
<script>


    var heightSVG = 700;
    var widthSVG = 700;
    d3.csv("data.csv",function(d){
        return d.value;
    },function(error,data){

        if(error)throw error;
                d3.select("body")
                .append("svg")
                .attr("width",widthSVG)
                .attr("height",heightSVG)
                .style("background","black");
```

Now save and run the file.

When we are not getting any output, it means our program has errors. You can identify in the browser console checking any error of the program. Go to browser console by right click on the browser page and hit 'Inspect'. It opens a console window. At the right hand corner it shows the errors. Here, you can identify that it is showing svg is not defined. Following this input, we check the program and add the missing SVG.

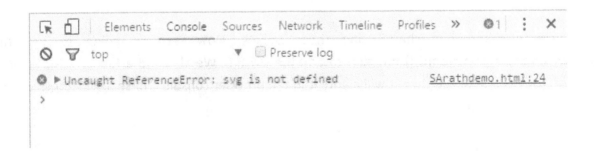

Fix the error and run the file.

```
var heightSVG = 700;
var widthSVG = 700;
d3.csv("data.csv",function(d){
    return d.value;
},function(error,data){

    if(error)throw error;
    var svg= d3.select("body")
            .append("svg")
            .attr("width",widthSVG)
            .attr("height",heightSVG)
            .style("background","black");


    svg.selectAll()
```

Code for data.csv

"value"

10

20

30

40

20

10

100

Code for D3DataLoad.html

```
<!DOCTYPE html>
<meta charset="utf-8">
<title>Adding attributes and selection to SVG element</title>
<link rel="stylesheet" type="text/css" href="style.css"></link>

<body>
```

```
<script src="../D3/d3.v3.min.js"></script>
<script>


    var heightSVG = 700;
    var widthSVG = 700;
    d3.csv("data.csv",function(d){
        return d.value;
    },function(error,data){

        if(error)throw error;
        var svg= d3.select("body")
            .append("svg")
            .attr("width",widthSVG)
            .attr("height",heightSVG)
            .style("background","black");

        svg.selectAll()
        .data(data)
        .enter()
        .append("rect")
        .attr("height",function(d,i){
            return d*100;
        })
        .attr("width","20px")
        .style("fill","orange")
        .attr("y",function(d,i){
            return heightSVG -(d)*10 ;
        })
        .attr("x",function(d,i){
            return i*40;
```

```
            });

        });
```

```
</script>
</body>
</html>
```

Output for the program

The output shows the bar chart corresponding data.csv file. In this output we can note that the final value is not fitting inside our SVG. To fix that, we will use scales. You can see this example in next section.

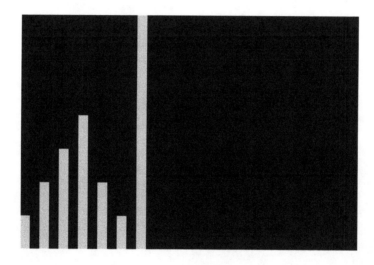

You can also check our **Learn D3.JS Hands-on And The Simple Way** video course for accelerated learning: <u>here</u> or use the below QR code for 50-90% off.

Learn D3.JS Hands-on And The Simple Way

UI5 Community Network • SAP Experts - SAP Services, SAP Consulting, SAP Education

Learn how to work with D3 Javascript libraries in step-by-step and most simple manner with lots of hands-on examples

⊙ 35 lectures   ⏱ 7 hours   ⌷⌷⌷ All Levels

★ ★ ★ ★ ★ 4.4
(10 ratings)

9. Scale and Axis

In the previous example we saw that our last rectangle bar is out of our SVG. To rectify this error we are using scales in our D3.

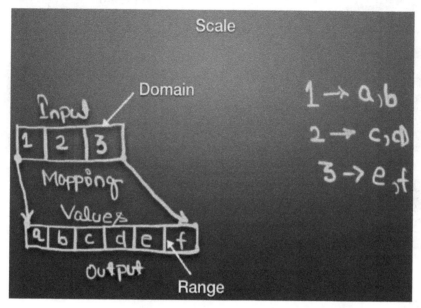

Generally we have an input and we have to map that input to the desired output. The output can be width of the canvas or the height of the canvas. Input can be our data points or how many numbers of data points we have to map. In D3 the input is called **domain** and the output is called **range**. So, we have to map the domain into range. For example, let's assume we have three inputs 1, 2, 3 and we have to map these three inputs with six alphabets namely a, b, c, d, e, f. One simple approach we will do here is we can assign each input value to two alphabets. That is 1 is having a and b, 2 is having c and d, 3 is having e and f. This is the simple example for how the mapping can be done. There can be multiple approaches like value based approach. Example 1 will have a, 2 will have b and c, 3 will have d, e, f.

In D3 we have two main types of scaling called **Linear** scaling and **Ordinal** Scaling.

Linear Scaling - It is for continuous input domains, such as numbers.

Ordinal Scaling - It is for discrete domain, such as a set of names or categories.

Ordinal scale

Let's take an example for the bar chart. In that bar chart if we want to place the bars at a proper distance from each other as shown in the picture below as 2, 4 and 6 units. In this data set we have input data set as [1, 2, 3] and we need to have an output data set as [2, 4, 6] that is how much distance it has from origin. In this scenario, we need to have a function to take each input data set and map it to the output data set. This function is called an ordinal scale.

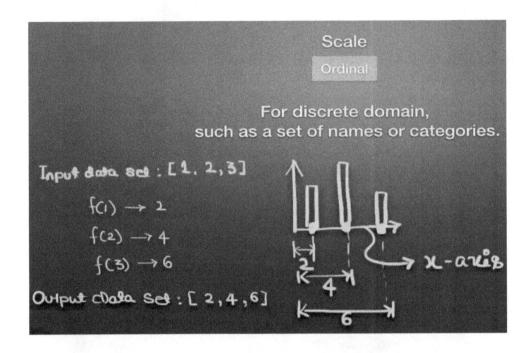

9.1. Linear Scale

These scales are used for continuous input domains, such as numbers. For example, if the input data set is [7, 10, 6], the entire canvas height is 100. We need to plot the graph within this 100 value. To plot the graph according to the canvas we need the output data set as 70, 100 and 60 units respectively for our input data sets.

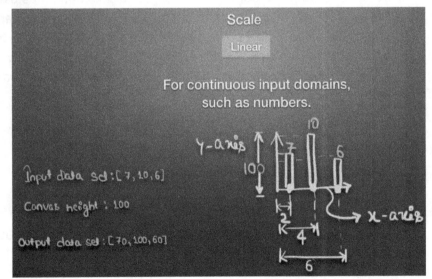

Syntax

Linear Scale

```
var y = d3.scale.linear().domain([0,d3.max(data)])   /* Min and Max value of data */
      .range([0, heightSVG]);            /* Specify the range to crate chart in specified area
```

9.2. Ordinal Scale

```
var x = d3.scale.ordinal().domain(d3.range(data.length)) /* Specify the no. of data points
      .rangeRoundBands([0,widthSVG]);  /* Creates range bands depending on widthSVG
```

We will use this scaling in example that we saw previously to resolve the issue of bar extending outside SVG. Create a new file (D3Scale.html) and copy the code into it. The change we need to do is adding a scale to it. For y axis we use the linear scale.

To use this x scale we need to replace the return value as return x(i); Here we are passing the index value that is going to be iterated through. It will return the corresponding x location that the bar should be drawn. After these changes made we run the application.

Coding

```
<!DOCTYPE html>
<meta charset="utf-8">
<title>Adding attributes and selection to SVG element</title>
<link rel="stylesheet" type="text/css" href="style.css"></link>


<body>
<script src="../D3/d3.v3.min.js"></script>
<script>

  var data=[10,20,30,40,100];
  var heightSVG = 700;
  var widthSVG = 700;


  var y = d3.scale.linear().domain([0,d3.max(data)])
        .range([0, heightSVG]); /* Y scale */
```

```javascript
var x = d3.scale.ordinal().domain(d3.range(data.length))
      .rangeRoundBands([0,widthSVG]);  /* X Scale */


var svg = d3.select("body")
      .append("svg")
      .attr("width",widthSVG)
      .attr("height",heightSVG)
      .style("background","black");

      svg.selectAll()
      .data(data)
      .enter()
      .append("rect")
      .attr("height",function(d,i){
        return d*100;
      })
      .attr("width","20px")
      .style("fill","orange")
      .attr("y",function(d,i){
              return heightSVG - y(d); /* Rectangle start to draw from the returned value */
      })
      .attr("x",function(d,i){
                                  return i*40; /* Replacing x with index value*/
      });
  });
</script>
</body>
</html>
```

Note: If we remove the heightSVG from this code

```
.attr("y",function(d,i){

        return y(d);
```

Then the output will be reversed. That is the bars start showing from higher to the lower size.

Output

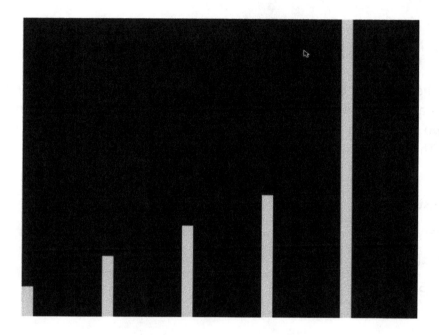

We can check this in console window also. To verify, right click on the browser window and select inspect element. Inside the console window enter the minimum data point value. In our case it is 10 so enter y(10) in the console window then it return 70. This 70 is our height of the first data set. Similarly we can check for y(100) then it will return 700. You can also check the x scale (ordinal scale) if we enter x(0) then it will return the padding left for the first rectangle because the bar starts without any padding. If we enter x(1) then it will return 140.

9.3. Axis

We use axis when we want to use scale in our graph. It helps user to understand the boundaries of data points and what is the value corresponds to. Generally in a two dimensional graph we are having two axis namely X – Axis and Y – Axis. To create an axis in D3 we use the function d3.svg.axis(). The actual syntax we create an Axis is

```
var yAxis = d3.svg.axis()
        .scale(y)
        .orient('left')
        .ticks(5);
```

We are using the function d3.svg.axis() and passing the scale to it. The orientation we are passing will tell the bar chart to be in left hand side. Ticks are used to have number of ticks we need in the Y- Axis. Similarly the syntax for X – Axis is

```
var xAxis = d3.svg.axis()
        .scale(x)
        .orient('bottom')
        .ticks(10);
```

We are passing the scale here. The orientation is given as bottom because we need the x axis comes under the bottom part of the bar chart. In our case we need more number of ticks. So we had given 10 as our parameter in ticks in X – Axis. Depending upon our requirements we can give more or less ticks. Generally in most cases we need more number of ticks in the X – Axis. We will see an example using this syntax in our cloud9 editor.

In the last example we created bar chart and introduced the concept of scale. In this section we will add axis to the bar chart. The first step we need to do is creating X - Axis and Y – Axis.

```
var yAxis = d3.svg.axis()
            .scale(y)
            .orient('left')
            .ticks(5);
```
①

```
var xAxis = d3.svg.axis()
            .scale(x)
            .orient('bottom')
            .ticks(5);
```
②

1. Adding Y – Axis with scale y, Orientation as left and ticks as 5.

2. Adding X – Axis with scale x, Orientation as bottom and ticks as 5.

```
var svg = d3.select("body")
        .append("svg")
        .attr("width",widthSVG)
        .attr("height",heightSVG)
        .style("transform","translate("+paddingChart+"px,"+paddingChart+"px")
        .style("background","black");
```
③

3. We are introducing two new axes. So we need some space display the axis. To perform that we need to add transform property into our SVG. The paddingChart variable is already defined initially as 40px.

4. Next we need to call our axis. To perform that we use the function .call(yAxis) similarly for X – Axis .call(xAxis). Here the 'g' element represents to group our axis and stroke is to add the colour of our axis as White.

```
svg.append("g")
.call(yAxis)
.style("stroke","#fff");

svg.append("g")
.call(xAxis)
.style("stroke","#fff");
```
④

After adding these if we run the code. We will see the result look like this

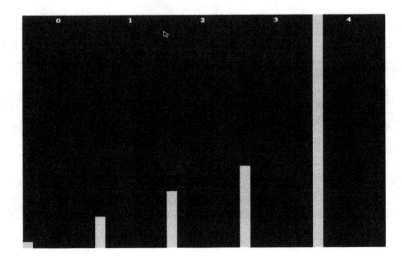

This is not the exact result we want. The Y- Axis is not visible and X – Axis at upper side.

5. First we push the X – Axis to the bottom side and then Y – Axis to little right hand side. To perform this we add the transform property here with value as translate. We added a variable axisMargin to generalize the axis margins. We need to declare the value as 30 in the declaration part.

```
svg.append("g")
.call(yAxis)
.attr("transform","translate("+axisMargin+",0)")
.style("stroke","#fff");

svg.append("g")
.call(xAxis)
.attr("transform","translate(0,"+(heightSVG-axisMargin)+")")
.style("stroke","#fff");
```

⑤

We fixed the axis now. However still, we need to move the chart to little up and right hand side. As of now if we run the code we will get the result as

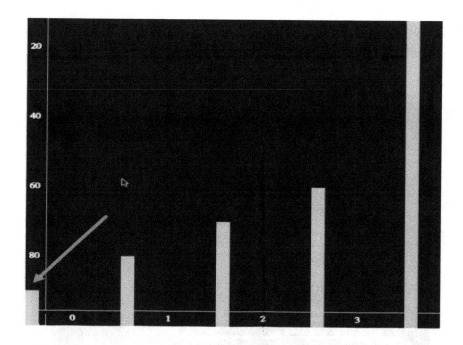

To fix the issue that shown by the arrow in that picture we need to add a simple CSS property.

6. First we will group the rectangle together by using an append function. Also we add the style function with class name as rectangle.

```
svg.append("g")
.attr("class","rectangle")
.selectAll()
.data(data)
.enter()
.append("rect")
.attr("height",function(d,i){
    return 0;
```

6

7. In the output we can see that the Y – Axis values are reversed. To fix that we need to reverse the range in Y – Axis.

```
var y = d3.scale.linear().domain([0,d3.max(data)])
    .range([heightSVG-axisMargin,0]);

var x = d3.scale.ordinal().domain(d3.range(data.length))
    .rangeRoundBands([0,widthSVG]);
```

7

If we replace the values heightSVG; and y(d); vice versa we can see the bar chart will get reversed. That is high to low and low to high.

```
svg.append("g")
.attr("class","rectangle")
.selectAll()
.data(data)
.enter()
.append("rect")
.attr("height",function(d,i){
    return heightSVG;
})
.attr("width","20px")
.style("fill","orange")
.attr("y",function(d,i){
    return y(d);
})
```

These are the changes we need to do for creating and aligning the axis. We need to do lots of experiments to get our correct result.

Code for D3Axis.html

```html
<!DOCTYPE html>
<meta charset="utf-8">
<title>Adding attributes and selection to SVG element</title>
<link rel="stylesheet" type="text/css" href="style.css"></link>


<body>
<script src="../D3/d3.v3.min.js"></script>
<script>

    var data=[10,20,30,40,100];
    var heightSVG = 700;
    var widthSVG = 700;
    var padding = 10;
```

```javascript
var paddingText = 30;
var paddingChart = 40;
var axisMargin = 30;
var margin = {

    'top':5,
    'right':20,
    'bottom':20,
    'left':50
};

var y = d3.scale.linear().domain([0,d3.max(data)])
    .range([heightSVG-axisMargin,0]);

var x = d3.scale.ordinal().domain(d3.range(data.length))
    .rangeRoundBands([0,widthSVG]);

var yAxis = d3.svg.axis()
        .scale(y)
        .orient('left')
        .ticks(5);

var xAxis = d3.svg.axis()
        .scale(x)
        .orient('bottom')
        .ticks(5);


var svg = d3.select("body")
        .append("svg")
        .attr("width",widthSVG)
```

```
.attr("height",heightSVG)
.style("transform","translate("+paddingChart+"px,"+paddingChart+"px")
.style("background","black");



svg.append("g")
.call(yAxis)
.attr("transform","translate("+axisMargin+",0)")
.style("stroke","#fff");


svg.append("g")
.call(xAxis)
.attr("transform","translate(0,"+(heightSVG-axisMargin)+")")
.style("stroke","#fff");



svg.append("g")
.attr("class","rectangle")
.selectAll()
.data(data)
.enter()
.append("rect")
.attr("height",function(d,i){
    return heightSVG;
})
.attr("width","20px")
.style("fill","orange")
.attr("y",function(d,i){
    return y(d);
})
```

```
</script>
</body>
</html>
```

Style.css

```css
.blueBack{

    background : blue;

}


.rectangle{
    transform: translate(30px,-30px) !important;
}
```

Output

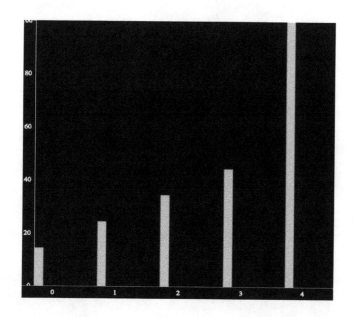

You can also check our **Learn D3.JS Hands-on And The Simple Way** video course for accelerated learning: <u>here</u> or use the below QR code for 50-90% off.

Learn D3.JS Hands-on And The Simple Way

UI5 Community Network • SAP Experts - SAP Services, SAP Consulting, SAP Education

Learn how to work with D3 Javascript libraries in step-by-step and most simple manner with lots of hands-on examples

⊕ 35 lectures   ⊙ 7 hours   ⦀ All Levels

★★★★★ 4.4
(10 ratings)

10. Events

Events are used to perform some action while we move the mouse over an object. For example, in the bar chart we created previously if we move the mouse over the bar then a small pop up will appear on it to display the value of the bar. Similarly when the bars are being generated then there will be some transition effects. These are done by using events. To create an event we need an on function. In this event we are using mouseover event. So we need to give the value as mouseover event inside the on function. The second parameter function(d) used to call the function during the function is triggered. To add a transition property during the bar is generated we need to use the function transition function with parameters duration of animation and its attributes to be changed in this transition. Example, while the bar start to generate it will generate from the bottom or sliding over from the side. These will be done by the attributes. Let's go to our cloud9 IDE to use events in our bar chart.

In last section we created the bar chart. Now we are going to use events to that bar chart.

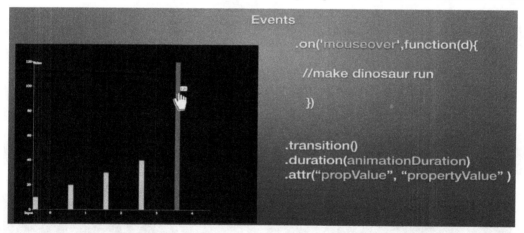

1. We need a tooltip to display the value of the bar. So we create a box and add a tooltip. Then we select the body. We append a div element. We need to add styling to the tooltip. We add the position as absolute and background as white colour. Also we added padding and border properties to the tooltip. The opacity we initially give 0 because we are going to hide this one for now. We can change it later by increasing the value.

```
var tooltip = d3.select('body')
                .append('div')
                .style('position','absolute')
                .style('background','#fff')
                .style('padding','5px 15px')
                .style('border','1px #fff solid')
                .style('opacity','0');
```

①

2. We are going to add on function for mouseover event. The function(d) will pull our tooltip while we move the mouse over the bar. The left and top are the positions to show the tooltip on the bar.

3. The d3.select(this).style('opacity',0.5); function will select the current bar that the mouse is pointing and it will reduce the opacity to 0.5. Once we reduced the opacity it will be set as 0.5 and does not change back to 1. To perform that we add another mouse over event to set it back to 1.

```
}).on('mouseover',function(d){

    tooltip.transition().style('opacity',1);
    tooltip.html(d)
    .style('left',(d3.event.pageX)+"px")
    .style('top',(d3.event.pageY)+"px");
```

②

```
    d3.select(this).style('opacity',0.5);

}).on('mouseout',function(d){

    d3.select(this).style('opacity',1);

});
```

③

4. The next step is to add transition effect. To perform that we add a transition function to the graph. We need to do the transition for all the rectangle so we selected all the rectangles by d3.SelectAll('rect'). The transition function is added and also the duration of transition effect added (Time in milliseconds). Also we need to add the attribute that is going to change.

```
d3.selectAll("rect").transition()
.duration(4000)
.attr('height',function(d,i){
    return heightSVG-y(d);
})
.attr('y',function(d,i){
    return y(d) ;
})
```
④

5. We need to start the height of the graph from 0 to the total height (heightSVG). For that we will change the y values.

```
svg.append("g")
.attr("class","rectangle")
.selectAll()
.data(data)
.enter()
.append("rect")
.attr("height",function(d,i){
    return 0;
})
.attr("width","20px")
.style("fill","orange")
.attr("y",function(d,i){
    return heightSVG ;
})
```
⑤

If we run these code after these changes then we will see the transition effects and tooltips.

Code for D3Axis.html

```
<!DOCTYPE html>
<meta charset="utf-8">
<title>Adding attributes and selection to SVG element</title>
<link rel="stylesheet" type="text/css" href="style.css"></link>


<body>
<script src="../D3/d3.v3.min.js"></script>
<script>
```

```
var data=[10,20,30,40,100];
var heightSVG = 700;
var widthSVG = 700;
var padding = 10;
var paddingText = 30;
var paddingChart = 40;
var axisMargin = 30;
var margin = {

  'top':5,
  'right':20,
  'bottom':20,
  'left':50
};


var y = d3.scale.linear().domain([0,d3.max(data)])
    .range([heightSVG-axisMargin,0]);


var x = d3.scale.ordinal().domain(d3.range(data.length))
    .rangeRoundBands([0,widthSVG]);


var yAxis = d3.svg.axis()
      .scale(y)
      .orient('left')
      .ticks(5);


var xAxis = d3.svg.axis()
      .scale(x)
      .orient('bottom')
      .ticks(5);
```

```
var svg = d3.select("body")
    .append("svg")
    .attr("width",widthSVG)
    .attr("height",heightSVG)
    .style("transform","translate("+paddingChart+"px,"+paddingChart+"px")
    .style("background","black");
var tooltip = d3.select('body')
    .append('div')
    .style('position','absolute')
    .style('background','#fff')
    .style('padding','5px 15px')
    .style('border','1px #fff solid')
    .style('opacity','0');
svg.append("g")
.call(yAxis)
.attr("transform","translate("+axisMargin+",0)")
.style("stroke","#fff");


svg.append("g")
.call(xAxis)
.attr("transform","translate(0,"+(heightSVG-axisMargin)+")")
.style("stroke","#fff");



svg.append("g")
.attr("class","rectangle")
.selectAll()
.data(data)
.enter()
```

```javascript
.append("rect")
.attr("height",function(d,i){
    return 0;
})
.attr("width","20px")
.style("fill","orange")
.attr("y",function(d,i){
    return heightSVG ;
})
.attr("x",function(d,i){
    return x(i);
}).on('mouseover',function(d){

    tooltip.transition().style('opacity',1);
    tooltip.html(d)
    .style('left',(d3.event.pageX)+"px")
    .style('top',(d3.event.pageY)+"px");

d3.select(this).style('opacity',0.5);

}).on('mouseout',function(d){

    d3.select(this).style('opacity',1);

});
d3.selectAll("rect").transition()
.duration(4000)
.attr('height',function(d,i){
    return heightSVG-y(d);
})
.attr('y',function(d,i){
```

```
            return y(d) ;
        })
</script>
</body>
</html>
```

Output

After 400ms

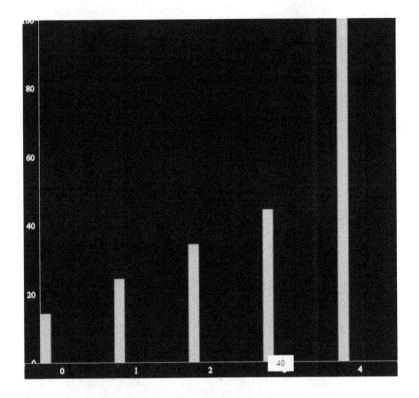

Note: This is transition effect and we can see the transition in the browser only. The pictures are only for demonstration purpose. To see the real transition effects, go to D3Axis.html file in the cloud9 editor and run the file.

File Name: D3Axis.html

Link:https://ide.c9.io/ajaytech/dataviz

You can also check our **Learn D3.JS Hands-on And The Simple Way** video course for accelerated learning: <u>here</u> or use the below QR code for 50-90% Off.

Learn D3.JS Hands-on And The Simple Way

UIS Community Network • SAP Experts · SAP Services, SAP Consulting, SAP Education

Learn how to work with D3 Javascript libraries in step-by-step and most simple manner with lots of hands-on examples

⏵ 35 lectures　🕐 7 hours　⦙⦙⦙ All Levels

★ ★ ★ ★ ★ 4.4
(10 ratings)

11. Bubble Chart

Bubble charts are the pretty nice ways to show correlation among the data points. For example consider the data points as shown below has X and Y Co-ordinates. While representing these data points using the bubble charts and there are some data points are grouped together. Those kinds of findings are very easy to find in bubble chart.

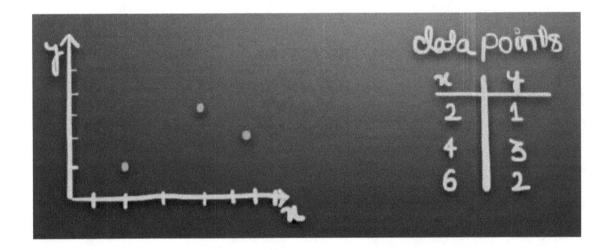

We may have extra dimension to our data like three dimensional data and we want to represent that in our graph. Then we will consider the 'd' as size of the circle. Depending upon the value of 'd' we can have bigger or smaller circles. So we can differentiate the data points not only in terms of positions in X and Y co-ordinates but also the size of the circle. Let's go to our cloud9 editor and start creating our bubble chart.

Previously we created bar chart with some transition effects. We are going to do some changes in the code to create a bar chart. To do that create a new file **D3Bubble.html** and copy the contents of **D3Axis.html** to perform some changes for bubble chart. Change the title name in the code to Bubble chart as we are coding for bubble chart.

1. The major change that we are going to change is from rectangle to circle.

   A. We need to change all the 'rect' class into 'circle'.

   B. We need radius 'r' to create a circle replace the height into radius 'r' here.

   C. Instead of 'y' and 'x' we need to change it to 'cy' and 'cx'

```
svg.append("g")
    .attr("class","circle")
    .selectAll()
    .data(dataVal1)
    .enter()
    .append("circle")
    .attr("r",function(d,i){
        return r(dataVal2[i]);
    })
    .attr("width","10px")
    .style("fill","orange")
    .attr("cy",function(d,i){
        return heightSVG ;
    })
    .attr("cx",function(d,i){
        return x(i);
```

A

B

C

2. Similarly we do changes in

    A. The transition part from 'rect' to 'circle'

    B. Function call from 'y' to 'cy'. We added the +px in return to take it as pixel
        instead of some other value.

```
d3.selectAll("circle").transition()
    .duration(4000)
    .attr('cy',function(d,i){
        return (y(d))+"px" ;
    })
```

A

B

We also need to change some CSS property. Since we created the CSS property for rectangle
only so we need to add circle in CSS to align the bubble chart from the correct axis. After this if
we run the code we will see the bubble chart with small radius.

```
.blueBack{

    background : blue;


}

.rectangle{
    transform: translate(30px,-30px) !important;
}

.circle{
    transform: translate(30px,0px) !important;



}
```

3. The next step is to add new dimensions to the bubble chart. To do that we will create object and hold the two keys namely 'val1' and 'val2'. The first key holds the same data and the second key holds the radius of the circle.

```
var data={
    "val1": [10,20,30,40,100],
    "val2":[20,30,50,40,70]};
```
③

4. As we changed the data values we also need to perform changes related to that. Also we need to add radius and define the Range round bands as minR and maxR ranges. For using this range round band we need to declare it in the declaration part.

```
var y = d3.scale.linear().domain([0,d3.max(dataVal1)])
        .range([heightSVG-axisMargin,0]);

var x = d3.scale.ordinal().domain(d3.range(dataVal1.length))
        .rangeRoundBands([0,widthSVG]);                          ④

var r = d3.scale.linear().domain([d3.min(dataVal2),d3.max(dataVal2)])
        .range([minR,maxR]);
```

We also updated the tooltip to display the radius as well.

```
tooltip.transition().style('opacity',1);
tooltip.html("y: "+d+" / r: "+dataVal2[i])
.style('left',(d3.event.pageX)+"px")
.style('top',(d3.event.pageY)+"px");
```

Code for D3Bubble.html

```html
<!DOCTYPE html>
<meta charset="utf-8">
<title>Bubble chart</title>
<link rel="stylesheet" type="text/css" href="style.css"></link>


<body>
<script src="../D3/d3.v3.min.js"></script>
<script>

  var data={
"val1": [10,20,30,40,100],
"val2":[20,30,50,40,70]};
  var heightSVG = 700;
  var widthSVG = 700;
  var padding = 10;
  var paddingText = 30;
  var paddingChart = 40;
  var axisMargin = 30;
  var margin = {

    'top':5,
    'right':20,
    'bottom':20,
    'left':50
```

```
};
var minR = 20;
var maxR = 70;
var dataVal1 = data["val1"];
var dataVal2 = data["val2"];

var y = d3.scale.linear().domain([0,d3.max(dataVal1)])
    .range([heightSVG-axisMargin,0]);

var x = d3.scale.ordinal().domain(d3.range(dataVal1.length))
    .rangeRoundBands([0,widthSVG]);

var r = d3.scale.linear().domain([d3.min(dataVal2),d3.max(dataVal2)])
    .range([minR,maxR]);

var yAxis = d3.svg.axis()
    .scale(y)
    .orient('left')
    .ticks(5);

var xAxis = d3.svg.axis()
    .scale(x)
    .orient('bottom')
    .ticks(5);

var svg = d3.select("body")
    .append("svg")
    .attr("width",widthSVG)
    .attr("height",heightSVG)
    .style("transform","translate("+paddingChart+"px,"+paddingChart+"px")
    .style("background","black");
```

```
var tooltip = d3.select('body')
        .append('div')
        .style('position','absolute')
        .style('background','#fff')
        .style('padding','5px 15px')
        .style('border','1px #fff solid')
        .style('opacity','0');

    svg.append("g")
    .call(yAxis)
    .attr("transform","translate("+axisMargin+",0)")
    .style("stroke","#fff");

     svg.append("g")
    .call(xAxis)
    .attr("transform","translate(0,"+(heightSVG-axisMargin)+")")
    .style("stroke","#fff");

    svg.append("g")
    .attr("class","circle")
    .selectAll()
    .data(dataVal1)
    .enter()
    .append("circle")
    .attr("r",function(d,i){
       return r(dataVal2[i]);
    })
    .attr("width","10px")
    .style("fill","orange")
    .attr("cy",function(d,i){
       return heightSVG ;
```

```
            })
            .attr("cx",function(d,i){
                return x(i);
            }).on('mouseover',function(d,i){

                tooltip.transition().style('opacity',1);
                tooltip.html("y: "+d+" / r: "+dataVal2[i])
                .style('left',(d3.event.pageX)+"px")
                .style('top',(d3.event.pageY)+"px");

                d3.select(this).style('opacity',0.5);

            }).on('mouseout',function(d){

                d3.select(this).style('opacity',1);

            });


            d3.selectAll("circle").transition()
            .duration(4000)
            .attr('cy',function(d,i){
                return (y(d))+"px" ;
            })
</script>
</body>
</html>
```

CSS Style

```
.blueBack{
```

```
    background : blue;


}


.rectangle{
    transform: translate(30px,-30px) !important;
}


.circle{
    transform: translate(30px,0px) !important;


}
```

Output

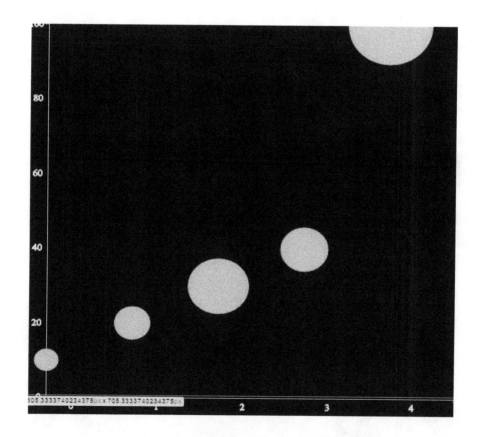

You can also check our **Learn D3.JS Hands-on And The Simple Way** video course for accelerated learning: <u>here</u> or use the below QR code for 50-90% off.

Learn D3.JS Hands-on And The Simple Way
UI5 Community Network • SAP Experts · SAP Services, SAP Consulting, SAP Education

Learn how to work with D3 Javascript libraries in step-by-step and most simple manner with lots of hands-on examples

⏵ 35 lectures   ⏱ 7 hours   ⦀ All Levels

★★★★★ 4.4
(10 ratings)

12. Pie Chart and Donut charts

Pie charts are used to show differentiation and comparison among data points. Most of the time in business context these are used to show percentage shares between different data point. Like revenues from different regions of our company or productions from different regions of factory. It can also be used to show some sales information of different regions that how they are performing in sales. We can come to a conclusion on the highest earning region and lowest earning regions. These are some of the examples that we are using pie chart. A slightly modified version of pie chart is donut chart. We can generate a donut chart by cutting out the inner circle of pie chart. To create a pie chart and donut chart we will use the following functions.

d3.svg.arc()

d3.layout.pie()

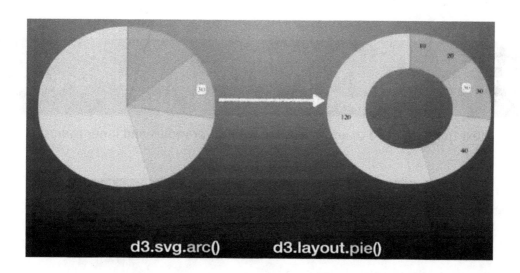

Let's go to our cloud9 editor and create the donut chart.

1. Simply create a file as D3PieChart.html and declare the variables and basic framework.

```
var padding = 1;
var paddingText = 30;
var paddingChart = 40;
var heightSVG = 700;
var widthSVG = 700;
var extraPadding = 200;
var animationDuration = 1000;
var animationDelay = 1000;
var radius = 200;
var innerRadius = 100;
var paddingPieX = 200;
var paddingPieY = 250;
var unit = "px";
```

2. Next we will add some data and colour scales. We use linear scale with domain parameters from 0 to maximum length of the data set. The colour values range from green to orange.

```
var data = [10,20,30,40,120];
var color = d3.scale.linear().domain([0,data.length])
             .range(["green","orange"]);
```

3. Next thing we need to add is the Arc with outer radius and inner radius.

```
var arc = d3.svg.arc()
          .outerRadius(radius)
          .innerRadius(innerRadius);
```

4. Next we need to create an arc label with outer and inner radius. The outer radius is subtracted from the paddingText.

```
var labelArc = d3.svg.arc()
             .outerRadius(radius-paddingText)
             .innerRadius(innerRadius-paddingText);
```

5. We are going to create a pie lay out in the next step. The following syntax will give us a pie layout.

```
var pie = d3.layout.pie()
            .sort(null)
            .value(function(d){return d;});
```

6. Creating SVG with maximum height and width of these SVG.

```
var svg = d3.select("body").append("svg")
        .attr("width",widthSVG+extraPadding)
        .attr("height",heightSVG+extraPadding)
        .style("background","#000");
```

7. Next we need to group all the SVG elements and then append the path of those elements. We are using a transform property here. This will align the chart to the browser window correctly. If we failed to introduce a transform property we won't be able to see the full chart inside the browser window.

```
var g = svg.selectAll(".arc")
        .data(pie(data))
        .enter()
        .append("g");

g.append("path")
        .attr("d",arc)
        .style("transform","translate("+paddingPieX+"px,"+paddingPieY+"px)")
        .style("fill",function(d,i){return "#000";})
```

As of now if we run the code we will able to see the donut chart. We still need to add label, tooltip and mouse over events to it.

8. To add a label we need to append a text with transformation to show this inside the arc. We use the translation property here to translate the X and Y co-ordinates. The centroid function we used here is to get a simple array which having X and Y values. We also add some extra padding using .attr("dy",".35em") function and .text(function(d){return d.value;});

```
g.append("text")
    .attr("transform",function(d){

        return "translate("+(parseInt(labelArc.centroid(d)[0])+paddingPieX-10)+","
        +(parseInt(labelArc.centroid(d)[1])+paddingPieY-10)+")";
    })
    .attr("dy",".35em")
    .text(function(d){return d.value;});
```

9. In the next step we are going to add some events to our donut chart. To do that we will use mouseover event and we will call the tooltip from there. The mouseover event will change the opacity to 0.5 and the mouseout event will set back to 1.

```
var tooltip = d3.select('body')
        .append('div')
        .style('position','absolute')
        .style('background','#fff')
        .style('padding','5px 15px')
        .style('border','1px #fff solid')
        .style('opacity','0');
```

```
g.on("mouseover",function(d){
    tooltip.transition()
    .style('opacity',1);

    tooltip.html(d.value)
    .style('left',(d3.event.pageX)+"px")
    .style('top',(d3.event.pageY)+"px")

    d3.select(this).style('opacity',0.5);

}).on("mouseout",function(){
        d3.select(this).style('opacity',1);
});
```

10. We can also use a transition function to show the donut chart in an animation while it starts to render.

```
d3.selectAll("path").transition()
.duration(animationDuration)
.style("transform","translate("+paddingPieX+"px,"+paddingPieY+"px)")
.style("fill",function(d,i){return color(i)});
```

Finally if we run this code then we will see the animation effect at start and if we move the mouse over it then it will show the tooltip with its corresponding values.

Code for DonutChart

```
<!DOCTYPE html>
<head>
</head>
<title>Pie chart</title>

<body >
<script src="../D3/d3.v3.min.js"></script>
<script >

var padding = 1;
var paddingText = 30;
var paddingChart = 40;
var heightSVG = 700;
var widthSVG = 700;
var extraPadding = 200;
var animationDuration = 1000;
var animationDelay = 1000;
var radius = 200;
var innerRadius = 100;
var paddingPieX = 200;
var paddingPieY = 250;
var unit = "px";
```

```
var data = [10,20,30,40,120];
var color = d3.scale.linear().domain([0,data.length])
        .range(["green","orange"]);


var arc = d3.svg.arc()
    .outerRadius(radius)
    .innerRadius(innerRadius);


var labelArc = d3.svg.arc()
        .outerRadius(radius-paddingText)
        .innerRadius(innerRadius-paddingText);


var pie = d3.layout.pie()
        .sort(null)
        .value(function(d){return d;});



var svg = d3.select("body").append("svg")
    .attr("width",widthSVG+extraPadding)
    .attr("height",heightSVG+extraPadding)
    .style("background","#000");

var tooltip = d3.select('body')
    .append('div')
    .style('position','absolute')
    .style('background','#fff')
    .style('padding','5px 15px')
    .style('border','1px #fff solid')
    .style('opacity','0');
```

```javascript
var g = svg.selectAll(".arc")
    .data(pie(data))
    .enter()
    .append("g");

    g.append("path")
    .attr("d",arc)
    .style("transform","translate("+paddingPieX+"px,"+paddingPieY+"px)")
    .style("fill",function(d,i){return "#000";})

g.append("text")
  .attr("transform",function(d){

    return "translate("+(parseInt(labelArc.centroid(d)[0])+paddingPieX-10)+","
    +(parseInt(labelArc.centroid(d)[1])+paddingPieY-10)+")";
  })
  .attr("dy",".35em")
  .text(function(d){return d.value;});


  g.on("mouseover",function(d){
    tooltip.transition()
    .style('opacity',1);

    tooltip.html(d.value)
    .style('left',(d3.event.pageX)+"px")
    .style('top',(d3.event.pageY)+"px")

    d3.select(this).style('opacity',0.5);
```

```
}).on("mouseout",function(){
    d3.select(this).style('opacity',1);
});

d3.selectAll("path").transition()
.duration(animationDuration)
.style("transform","translate("+paddingPieX+"px,"+paddingPieY+"px)")
.style("fill",function(d,i){return color(i)});


</script>
</body>


</html>
```

Output

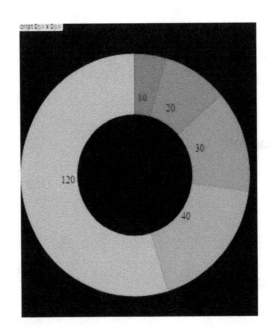

12.1. Converting Donut chart into Pie Chart

In the previous section we saw how to create donut chart. In this section we will see how to convert the donut chart into pie chart with a simple change. The only thing we need to do is to change the inner radius to 0.

```
var padding = 1;
var paddingText = 30;
var paddingChart = 40;
var heightSVG = 700;
var widthSVG = 700;
var extraPadding = 200;
var animationDuration = 1000;
var animationDelay = 1000;
var radius = 200;
var innerRadius = 0;
var paddingPieX = 200;
var paddingPieY = 250;
var unit = "px";
```

Code for D3PieChart.html

```
<!DOCTYPE html>
<head>
</head>
<title>Pie chart</title>

<body >
<script src="../D3/d3.v3.min.js"></script>
<script >

var padding = 1;
var paddingText = 30;
var paddingChart = 40;
var heightSVG = 700;
```

```
var widthSVG = 700;

var extraPadding = 200;

var animationDuration = 1000;

var animationDelay = 1000;

var radius = 200;

var innerRadius = 0;

var paddingPieX = 200;

var paddingPieY = 250;

var unit = "px";


var data = [10,20,30,40,120];
var color = d3.scale.linear().domain([0,data.length])
        .range(["green","orange"]);


var arc = d3.svg.arc()
    .outerRadius(radius)
    .innerRadius(innerRadius);


var labelArc = d3.svg.arc()
        .outerRadius(radius-paddingText)
        .innerRadius(innerRadius-paddingText);


var pie = d3.layout.pie()
        .sort(null)
        .value(function(d){return d;});


var svg = d3.select("body").append("svg")
    .attr("width",widthSVG+extraPadding)
    .attr("height",heightSVG+extraPadding)
```

```
        .style("background","#000");

var tooltip = d3.select('body')
    .append('div')
    .style('position','absolute')
    .style('background','#fff')
    .style('padding','5px 15px')
    .style('border','1px #fff solid')
    .style('opacity','0');



var g = svg.selectAll(".arc")
    .data(pie(data))
    .enter()
    .append("g");


    g.append("path")
    .attr("d",arc)
    .style("transform","translate("+paddingPieX+"px,"+paddingPieY+"px)")
    .style("fill",function(d,i){return "#000";})

g.append("text")
   .attr("transform",function(d){

    return "translate("+(parseInt(labelArc.centroid(d)[0])+paddingPieX-10)+","
    +(parseInt(labelArc.centroid(d)[1])+paddingPieY-10)+")";
   })
   .attr("dy",".35em")
   .text(function(d){return d.value;});
```

```
g.on("mouseover",function(d){
  tooltip.transition()
  .style('opacity',1);

  tooltip.html(d.value)
  .style('left',(d3.event.pageX)+"px")
  .style('top',(d3.event.pageY)+"px")

  d3.select(this).style('opacity',0.5);

}).on("mouseout",function(){
    d3.select(this).style('opacity',1);
});

d3.selectAll("path").transition()
.duration(animationDuration)
.style("transform","translate("+paddingPieX+"px,"+paddingPieY+"px)")
.style("fill",function(d,i){return color(i)});

</script>
</body>

</html>
```

Output

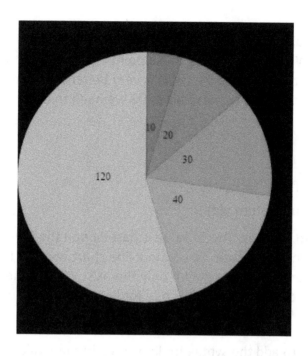

You can also check our **Learn D3.JS Hands-on And The Simple Way** video course for accelerated learning: here or use the below QR code for 50-90% off.

Learn D3.JS Hands-on And The Simple Way
UI5 Community Network • SAP Experts - SAP Services, SAP Consulting, SAP Education

Learn how to work with D3 Javascript libraries in step-by-step and most simple manner with lots of hands-on examples

★★★★★ 4.4
(10 ratings)

35 lectures   7 hours   All Levels

13. Line Chart

Line charts are wonderful ways to represent **trends over time**. It is like multiple small bubbles representing our data. We are connecting those points using straight line. When we have a lot of data points over time then using a line chart is very beneficial to see some of the patterns or trends over time. To create a simple line chart in D3 we need to use the function

d3.svg.line()

.x(function(d,i) { return x(i)})

.y(function(d){return return y(d) });

We are passing the x and y values. The 'x' value is based upon the index value 'i'. The 'y' value is based upon the data point value itself. To create a line chart we take the code for bar chart and removed the code for bars and made it with only the axis. We use the linear and ordinal scales we used in the bar chart. So we will add the code for line chart to draw using D3.

1. We are going to add the syntax for line and add the x value and y value with function having data and index. Here the y scale value may not return the integer value so we need to add parseInt to get integer value the data.

```
var line = d3.svg.line()
        .x(function(d,i){return x(i);})
        .y(function(d){return parseInt(y(d));});
```
1

2. We need to append the path to the svg. We are using a new function called datum to specify data. Also we will add the stroke attributes and add data to line. This will call the line function on each data points.

```
svg.append("path")
    .datum(data)
    .attr("stroke","orange")
    .attr("d",line)
```
2

After we have added these codes if we try to run this we will get the line that is connected according to the data points. Next we need to add a tooltip while we put the mouse over the line then it will show the corresponding 'y' value. In bar chart and bubble chart we have discrete values but in this case we will use continuous values so it will be tricky to show the values. This is because if we put the mouse over any part of the line it must show the corresponding 'y' values. So we need to find a way for it.

3. We will add a mouseover event for transition of tooltip.

```
.on("mouseover",function(d,i){
        tooltip.transition()
        .style("opacity",1);                3
```

4. We need to add a tooltip for the mouse event. As we told that it will be little tricky here. For that we are going to use a scale here. First we define the scale and then add the tooltip. To define scale we used hoverVal variable and defined the minimum and maximum range.

```
var hoverVal = d3.scale.linear().domain([0,heightSVG])
            .range([d3.max(data),0]);            4
```

5. Now we add the tooltip with the parameter hoverVal and get the y position. Also we will add the position of the tooltip to display on the line. So we define the tooltip style as left and top. The value 50 added to the chartBottomPadding is used to equalize the exact 'y' value to show in the tooltip.

```
tooltip.html(parseInt((hoverVal(d3.event.pageY-chartBottomPadding+50))))
        .style('left',(d3.event.pageX)+"px")
        .style('top',(d3.event.pageY)+"px");
                                                5
        d3.select(this).style("opacity",0.5);
```

6. As we created mouseover event we also need to create a mouseout event to change the event back to normal.

```
}).on("mouseout",function(){
                                        6
        d3.select(this).style("opacity",1);
})
```

Once we complete this we can run the program then we will get the line chart. In real scenarios the line chart is not the only chart present in our project. In those cases we have to do some calculations and adding some padding to it. We need to do lot of trial and error to reach our final result.

7. Additionally we can add some text property to tell what is the axis is about like amplitude, time, value and other variables. To do that we will append the text property to our 'x' and 'y' axis.

```
svg.append("g")
    //.attr("class","axis")
    .call(yAxis)
    .style("fill","none")
    .style("stroke","#fff")
    .append("text")
    .attr("transform","translate(-"+paddingText+",0)")
    .attr("dy","0.71rem")
    .style("text-anchor","end")
    .text("Value");
```

```
svg.append("g")
    .call(xAxis)
    .attr("transform", "translate(0,"+(heightSVG)+")")
    .style("fill","none")
    .style("stroke","#fff")
    .append("text")
    .attr("transform","translate(-"+paddingText+",0)")
    .attr("dy","0.71rem")
    .style("text-anchor","end")
    .text("Time");
```

Code for D3LineChart.html

```
<!DOCTYPE html>
<head>
<style>
```

```html
</style>
</head>
<title>Line chart</title>
<meta charset="utf-8">

<body >
<script src="../D3/d3.v3.min.js"></script>
<script >
 var padding = 1;
 var paddingText = 30;
 var paddingChart = 40;
var heightSVG = 700;
var widthSVG = 700;
var animationDuration = 1000;
var animationDelay = 1000;
var chartBottomPadding = 200;



var data = [10,20,30,40,120];



var svg = d3.select("body").append("svg").attr("width", widthSVG+200)
   .attr("height", heightSVG+chartBottomPadding)
   .style("transform", "translate("+paddingChart+"px,"+paddingChart+"px)")
   .style("padding-left","100px")
   .style("padding-top","100px")
   .style("background", "#000");

var tooltip = d3.select('body').append('div')
        .style('position','absolute')
        .style('background','#fff')
```

```
                .style('padding','5 15px')
                .style('border','1px #fff solid')
                .style('border-radius','5px')
                .style('opacity','0');


var y = d3.scale.linear().domain([0,d3.max(data)])
        .range([heightSVG,0]);

var hoverVal = d3.scale.linear().domain([0,heightSVG])
            .range([d3.max(data),0]);

var x = d3.scale.ordinal().domain(d3.range(data.length))
    .rangeRoundBands([0, widthSVG]);

var yAxis = d3.svg.axis()
    .scale(y)
    .orient("left")
    .ticks(5);
//.tickValues([1, 2, 3, 5, 8, 13]);;

var xAxis = d3.svg.axis()
    .scale(x)
    .orient("bottom")
    .ticks(10);

svg.append("g")
    //.attr("class","axis")
    .call(yAxis)
    .style("fill","none")
    .style("stroke","#fff")
```

```
      .append("text")
      .attr("transform","translate(-"+paddingText+",0)")
      .attr("dy","0.71rem")
      .style("text-anchor","end")
      .text("Value");


svg.append("g")
    .call(xAxis)
    .attr("transform", "translate(0,"+(heightSVG)+")")
    .style("fill","none")
    .style("stroke","#fff")
    .append("text")
    .attr("transform","translate(-"+paddingText+",0)")
    .attr("dy","0.71rem")
    .style("text-anchor","end")
    .text("Time");


var line = d3.svg.line()
        .x(function(d,i){return x(i);})
        .y(function(d){return parseInt(y(d));});


svg.append("path")
   .datum(data)
   .attr("stroke","orange")
   .attr("d",line)
   .on("mouseover",function(d,i){
     tooltip.transition()
     .style("opacity",1);

     tooltip.html(parseInt((hoverVal(d3.event.pageY-chartBottomPadding+50))))
          .style('left',(d3.event.pageX)+"px")
```

```
                    .style('top',(d3.event.pageY)+"px");


          d3.select(this).style("opacity",0.5);


   }).on("mouseout",function(){


      d3.select(this).style("opacity",1);

   })
```

</script>
</body>

</html>

Output

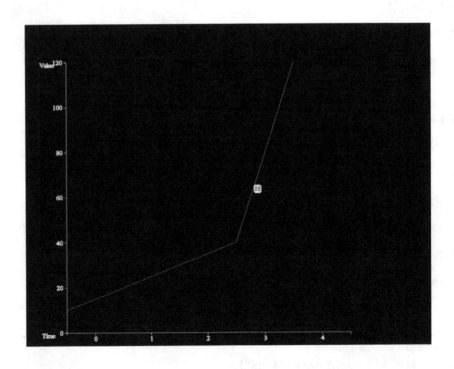

You can also check our **Learn D3.JS Hands-on And The Simple Way** video course for accelerated learning: here or use the below QR code for 50-90% off.

Learn D3.JS Hands-on And The Simple Way
UI5 Community Network • SAP Experts - SAP Services, SAP Consulting, SAP Education

Learn how to work with D3 Javascript libraries in step-by-step and most simple manner with lots of hands-on examples

35 lectures   7 hours   All Levels

★ ★ ★ ★ ★ 4.4
(10 ratings)

14. Maps

Maps are one of the most exciting and interesting data representation formats. While we see a map representation we can have a question how we can create a map. In this example we will create a simple US map. This US map consists of many numbers of states and each state is having a polygon shape.

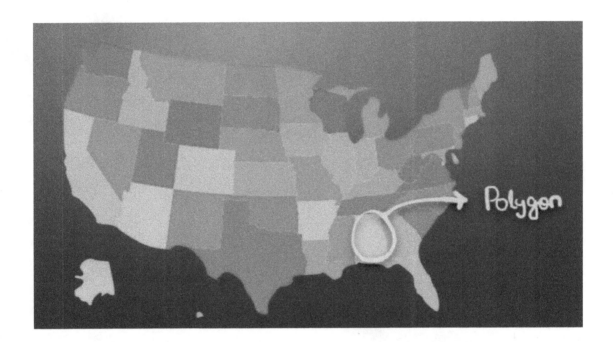

While we look into the polygon we can see that what are the corresponding 'X' and 'Y' coordinates involved that represents the boundary. For example if we consider 'n' number of points that 'n' can be 100 or 20 or 10. Then each point joint sequentially will result into closed boundary that represents a state. All the points of coordinates are a list of array. This is the first thing we need to know to create a polygon. Also we need to know some basic property of the state like name of the state and id of the state. These two data combined normally called Geo-JSON data. We will see the Geo-JSON data in detail in the example. Apart from these another thing we need to create a map is projections. This is because while we use geometrical we need to consider the earth is spherical in shape. When we are representing a 3D data format into 2D then we need to go with projections.

 D3 provides many popular formats for projecting these 3D data into 2D. Let's look into some of the projections we used in our project.

Now we go to the link https://github.com/d3/d3/wiki/Geo-Projections and see there are lot of geo projections formats and select one that we are going to use it in our project. Each one has some specific benefits. We are going to use the **d3.geo.albersUsa** format.

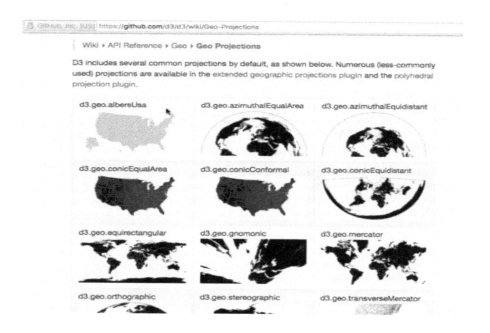

Now we can move to our coding part using cloud9 editor. Let we see the GeoJSON data before going to actual development.

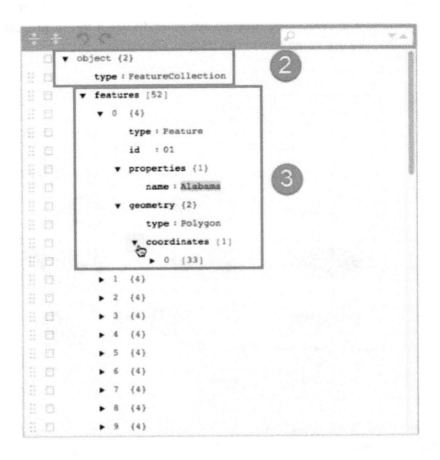

1. The GeoJSON data is a very big data representation. There are lot of coordinates and lot of information.

2. The top level represented in the picture is having an object of this GeoJSON data representation format. If we go one level inside it then we can see that the object is having two keys as type and features. Type represents the type of GeoJSON data it corresponds.

3. The feature is actually an array of objects. If we open any one of the individual objects then we can see the type, id, properties and geometry as keys. The property will represent the name of the state. The geometry represents the coordinates of the polygon in the states corresponds to.

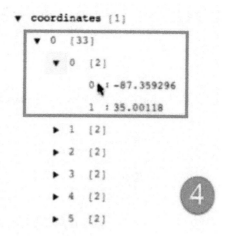

4. We can see a lot of coordinates. The '0' is the coordinate for the state Alabama and it contains 33 coordinates. If we still extend it we can see the '0th' and '1st' index of the coordinates. The '0th' index represent 'X' and '1st' index value represents 'Y'. Most of the time the GeoJSON data will available on internet to download and work on them.

"You can also check our **Learn D3.JS Hands-on And The Simple Way** video course for accelerated learning: <u>here</u> or use the below QR code for 50-90% off."

Learn D3.JS Hands-on And The Simple Way

UI5 Community Network • SAP Experts · SAP Services, SAP Consulting, SAP Education

Learn how to work with D3 Javascript libraries in step-by-step and most simple manner with lots of hands-on examples

⏵ 35 lectures   🕐 7 hours   ⋮⋮⋮ All Levels

★ ★ ★ ★ ★ 4.4
(10 ratings)

15. Final Project

In this section we are going to start working in our final project and we will see how we will use D3 in real project. In this we will work in a data visualization project and **visualizing data is one of the hot skill sets in the market place right now**. If you want to learn more about data visualization then we will highly recommend to check our '**Learn Data Visualization in 7 simple steps**' course in Udemy. This will provide a very firm basic understanding of how to work in a data visualization project. In the next section we are going to see the use case to work in D3.

Before starting any data visualization project we should always have clear purpose statement/requirements. Let's look into the purpose statement that we have here.

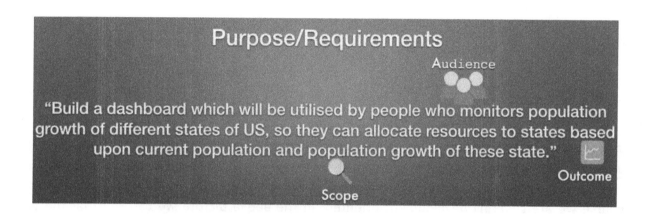

According to this purpose statement we have to build a dashboard that will be utilized by **people who monitors population growth** of different states of US, so they can **allocate resources to states** based upon **current population and population growth of these states.**

Here we can see the three main parts

- Who is the audience?
- What is the scope?
- Outcome

Audience: People who monitors population. We are going to create visualization project for them using D3.

Scope and Outcome: Using this visualization they will be allocating the resources to those states according to this.

Once we are clear on what we are going to do in a data visualization project then we will go into the 7 steps of data visualization project. Initial stage we will acquire the data and times after we will spend time in parsing the data and preparing it for usage.

This is the wireframe based upon our requirement that we already created in moqups website. We have skipped how to acquire data and how to work with data, filtering and creating this wireframe because, we covered these 7 steps in our other courses of data visualization. This course we are covering development oriented. In the above picture we can see that the bar chart with population of all the state and we also have a USA map. The KPI field shows the data of the population of current state.

There is also a small bar chart above our map that will show the variation of population for that particular years will be mentioned. This is an interactive D3 map that if we press any state on the map and the KPI values and Small bar chart will change corresponding to the data.

15.1. Code Structure

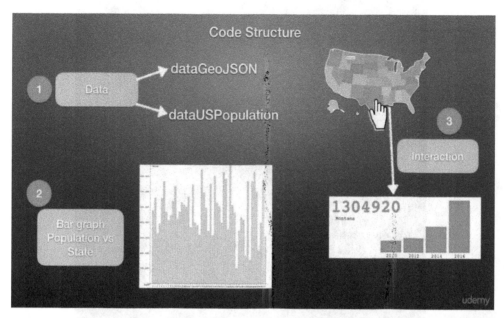

1. Let's see the code structure to solve the use case that we discussed. The first thing is the GeoJSON data file for our USA map. The second thing is the data for US population. These two are the JSON data that will be given to us before starting the project.

2. Next we need to create the bar chart for population vs graph of all states of US.

3. The third step is to add the interaction event. If we press on any single state of the map then we should be able to see the bar chart that represents the population of that state over years. We also update the KPI field information based upon the state we have selected. Next we will see these steps in our coding using cloud9 editor.

15.2. Creating map project

1. Create a new file and name it as D3FinalProject.html and copy the content of the map that we got from the github and paste it in the file. We will see a very big geoJSON data and minimize/collapse it to see other codes easily.

```
    var data = {
"type": "FeatureCollection",
"features": [
  {
    "type": "Feature",
    "id": "01",
    "properties": {
      "name": "Alabama"
    },
    "geometry": {
      "type": "Polygon",
      "coordinates": [
        [
          [
            -87.359296,
            35.00118
          ],
          [
            -85.606675,
            34.984749
          ],
          [
            -85.431413,
            34.124869
          ],
```

```
var data = {    };
```

2. Next we need the population data of US. We can see the JSON data for population of US. It contains huge number of data and each object is having a name key field and we have the data for the year 2010, 2012, 2014 and 2016. These are even number of years that we are going to use. While we are in real projects we are capturing the data from web services or reading the data from some files. The purpose of this use case is simple here so we can use the hard coded data inside our D3 program. We will copy the JSON data and paste it inside var dataUSPopulation = [{<data to be pasted here>}];

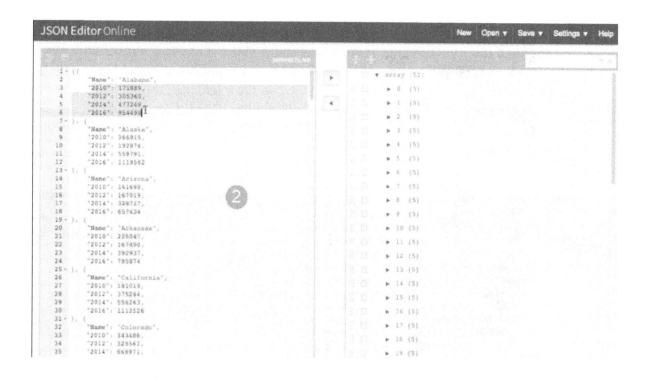

3. Other remaining things are same for the map. We will increase the width and height and also we add some padding to the graph.

```
//Width and height
var w = 1600;
var h = 800;
var margin ={

    left:32,
    right:30,
    bottom:30,
    top:30
};
var numOfState = 50;
var scaleOfMap = 1000;
var tooltip = d3.select('body').append('div')
        .style('position','absolute')
        .style('background','#fff')
        .style('padding','5 15px')
        .style('border','1px #fff solid')
        .style('border-radius','5px')
        .style('opacity','0');
```

4. In the map we also have a click event. That is whenever a user click a particular state on the map the user can able to see a bar chart. We will execute a function while the click event occurs. We can see that we are using two functions that we are using here update and new. The new function will call while the user clicks the state for first time. On that time the state population graph will appear. Once it appears and user clicks any other state the update function will be called. The 'if' statement should be added after creating state bar chart.

```
}).on("click", function(d,i){

    if(document.getElementById("stateBar").childNodes.length>0)
    {
        addStateBarChart(d,i,"update");
    }else{
        addStateBarChart(d,i,"new");
    }
```

15.3. Defining properties for our state vs population bar chart

5. Next we are going to define the state vs population bar chart (Main bar chart) . To do that we will create a function called barFirstTimeRender(). We will create the limit of bar chart and other boundaries and padding. Also copy the tooltip of the map and use it here. The maxPop is used to fix the highest population of all the states and use that for scaling.

6. We use the 'for loop' to find the maximum population value of the current year. If(!Number.isNaN(parseInt(k))){ - This is used to allow only year values inside the key condition. For that we used 'not a number(NaN)' is used.

```
function barFirstTimeRender(){

    var maxPop = 0;
    var widthBar = 750;
    var heightBar = 700;
    var paddingText = 70;
  var tooltip = d3.select('body').append('div')
            .style('position','absolute')
            .style('background','#fff')
            .style('padding','5 15px')
            .style('border','1px #fff solid')
            .style('border-radius','5px')
            .style('opacity','0');
```

⑤

```
    for(var i=0;i<dataUSPopulation.length;i++){
        for(k in dataUSPopulation[i]){
            if(!Number.isNaN(parseInt(k))){

                if(dataUSPopulation[i][k]>maxPop){
                    maxPop = dataUSPopulation[i][k];
                }
            }
        }
    }
```

⑥

7. Once we have the maximum population that will be the upper limit for the bar chart then we will create the scales.

```
var h = d3.scale.linear()
        .domain([0,maxPop])
        .range([0,heightBar]);

var y = d3.scale.linear()
         .domain([0,maxPop])
        .range([heightBar,0]);

var x = d3.scale.ordinal()
        .domain(d3.range(dataUSPopulation.length))
        .rangeRoundBands([0,widthBar]);
```

⑦

8. After creating scales we will create the 'Y' Axis with number of ticks, orientation and scale. Similarly for 'X' axis also. Also we will create the width of the bar by dividing widthBar / dataUSPopulation with floor value to make sure a complete rounded value.

```
var yAxis = d3.svg.axis()
            .scale(y)
            .orient('left')
            .ticks(10);

var xAxis = d3.svg.axis()
            .scale(x)
            .orient('bottom')
            .ticks(50);

var widthOfBar = Math.floor(widthBar / dataUSPopulation.length)-1;
```

8

9. We will group 'Y' axis and 'X' axis separately because we will apply the CSS property separately.

```
svg.append("g")
    .attr("id","yAxis")
    .call(yAxis)
    .style("stroke","#000")
    .attr("transform","translate("+paddingText+",0)");

svg.append("g")
    .attr("id","xAxis")
    .call(xAxis)
    .style("stroke","#000")
    .attr("transform","translate("+paddingText+","+(heightBar)+")");
```

9

10. Next we will append the 'Y' axis and 'X' Axis to our SVG for this bar chart. We are plotting the bar here.

```
var plot = svg.append("g")
        .attr("id","barPlot")
        .selectAll()
        .data(dataUSPopulation)
        .enter()
        .append("rect")
        .attr("width",widthOfBar)
        .attr("height",function(d,i){        10


            return h(d["2016"]);
        })
        .style("fill","orange")
        .attr("y",function(d,i){
            return heightBar- h(d["2016"]);
        })
        .attr("x",function(d,i){
            return x(i);
```

11. Until this if we run the code we will be getting the bar chart. We have to call the barFirstTimeRender function so call it before the function we created. We can also add a tool tip event using the mouse over event.

```
}).on('mouseover',function(d){

  tooltip.transition()
      .style('opacity',1);
    tooltip.html("2016 : "+d["2016"]+" "+d["Name"])
        .style('left',(d3.event.pageX)+"px")
        .style('top',(d3.event.pageY)+"px");

      d3.select(this).style('opacity',0.5);        11

})
.on('mouseout',function(){

    d3.select(this).style('opacity',1);

});
```

15.4. Defining properties for our individual state vs Year bar chart

12. The next step will be the State vs Year bar chart that needs to be display while clicking any of the state. We already saw that we have two functions that we are

going to use 'update' and 'new'. So we will come back to our addStateBarChart() function to continue plotting our State vs Year population chart. We will be using small renamed variables used here to differentiate the main bar chart variables and these bar chart variables.

```
function addStateBarChart(data,index,mode){

    var sBMaxPop = 0;
    var sBWidthBar = 400;
    var sBHeightBar = 250;
    var sBPaddingText = 10;
    var sTtooltip = d3.select('body').append('div')
            .style('position','absolute')
            .style('background','#fff')
            .style('padding','5 15px')
            .style('border','1px #fff solid')
            .style('border-radius','5px')
            .style('opacity','0');
```
(12)

13. We are using the sBData here. Here the data is different. We will select one particular state and draw bar chart for that. Each individual state is having a different index. This index will be passed to the function parameter. We also create a new sBDataNew array to store the Year value into it to make the process easier.

```
var sBData = dataUSPopulation[index];
var sBDataNew = [];
var sBNumYear = 0;
var sBState = dataUSPopulation[index]["Name"];

for(k in sBData){
    if(!Number.isNaN(parseInt(k))){

        sBNumYear++;
        sBDataNew.push({

            "year":k,
            "popl":sBData[k]
        });

        if(sBMaxPop < sBData[k]){
            sBMaxPop = sBData[k];
        }
    }
};
```
(13)

14. Next we will define the scales for the bar chart and also the width of the bar.

```
var sBH = d3.scale.linear().domain([0,sBMaxPop])
            .range([0,sBHeightBar]);

var sBY = d3.scale.linear().domain([0,sBMaxPop])
            .range([sBHeightBar,0]);

var sBX = d3.scale.ordinal().domain(d3.range(sBNumYear))  (14)
            .rangeRoundBands([0,sBWidthBar]);


var sBWidthOfBar =  Math.floor(sBWidthBar / sBNumYear)-1;
```

15. If the bar chart is new and it will start render that if we click the bar chart for the first time. The mode new is the third parameter of the function of this small bar chart. We will create a global variable called statePlot variable and use it inside the mode.

```
if(mode === "new"){

    statePlot.selectAll()
    .data(sBDataNew)
    .enter()
    .append("rect")
    .attr("width",sBWidthOfBar)
    .attr("height",function(d,i){            (15)
        return parseInt(sBH(d["popl"]));
    })
    .attr("y",function(d,i){

        return parseInt(sBY(d["popl"]));
    })
    .attr("x",function(d,i){

        return sBX(i);
    })
```

```
.style("fill","green").on('mouseover',function(d){

    tooltip.transition()
      .style('opacity',1);
      tooltip.html(d["year"]+" : "+d["pop1"])
        .style('left',(d3.event.pageX)+"px")
        .style('top',(d3.event.pageY)+"px");

      d3.select(this).style('opacity',0.5);

})
.on('mouseout',function(){

    d3.select(this).style('opacity',1);

});
```

16. In the else if part we write the code to update the data. This will make the transitions and display the graph for the current state.

```
}else if(mode === "update"){
    statePlot.selectAll("rect")
    .data(sBDataNew)
    .transition()
    .duration(1000)
    .attr("width",sBWidthOfBar)
    .attr("height",function(d,i){
        return parseInt(sBH(d["pop1"]));
    })
    .attr("y",function(d,i){

        return parseInt(sBY(d["pop1"]));
    })
    .attr("x",function(d,i){

        return sBX(i);
    })
    .style("fill","green");


}else{

    return ;
}
```

15.5. Defining and Drawing KPI numbers

17.   The final part is defining the KPI numbers as per our use case. This will display the data for the particular state We will add the KPI inside the addBarChart() function.

```
svg.selectAll("#kpi")
.text(sBData["2016"])
.transition()
.duration(1000);


svg.selectAll("#kpiDec")
.text(sBState)
.transition()
.duration(1000);
```
(17)

18. We also need to add the KPI information to the function barFirstTimeRender function.

```
svg.append("text")
.attr("id","kpi")
.text("State Population")
.attr("class","KPIMain")
.attr("x",parseInt(widthBar/2 - 200))
.attr("y",parseInt(heightBar/2 - 200));

svg.append("text")
.attr("id","kpiDec")
.text("State Name")
.attr("class","KPIDesc")
.attr("x",parseInt(widthBar/2 - 200))
.attr("y",parseInt(heightBar/2 - 200));
```
(18)

15.6. CSS and Other Small Changes

19. Without CSS the map will not look good. All the map and charts will be not aligned properly. To fix that we need to add the CSS styles to correct the elements.

Without CSS

So we need to improve the CSS. After we did some trial and error finally we have a proper CSS to display our project correctly.

```css
<style type="text/css">
  /* No style rules here yet */

  g#barPlot {
          transform: translateX(70px) !important;
      }

      .KPIMain{
          transform:translate(814px,-82px);
          font-size:72px;
          fill:gray !important;
          font-weight:bold;
      }
      .KPIDesc{
          transform:translate(840px,-41px);
          font-size:20px;
          fill:gray !important;
      }
      .map{
          transform:translate(400px,77px);

      }
</style>
```

19

Code for D3FinalProject.html is available in the repository https://c9.io/ajaytech/dataviz

It contains 15000+ lines of code that can't able to share here. So go to the repository and verify your coding.

15.7 Output

You can also check our **Learn D3.JS Hands-on And The Simple Way** video course for accelerated learning: here or use the below QR code for 50-90% off.

Learn D3.JS Hands-on And The Simple Way

UI5 Community Network • SAP Experts · SAP Services, SAP Consulting, SAP Education

Learn how to work with D3 Javascript libraries in step-by-step and most simple manner with lots of hands-on examples

⚫ 35 lectures   🕐 7 hours   ⦀ All Levels

★ ★ ★ ★ ★ 4.4
(10 ratings)

Reference and bibliography

- http://alignedleft.com/work/d3-book : Interactive Data Visualization for the Web by Scott Murray
- https://d3js.org/: D3 JavaScript Libraries official documentation and API reference.
- http://www.census.gov/ : US Census government website for public data to show use case.

www.ingramcontent.com/pod-product-compliance
Lightning Source LLC
Chambersburg PA
CBHW080556060326
40689CB00021B/4877